Random Memories We Left Behind

JEANETTA CLENTON

WESTBOW
PRESS®
A DIVISION OF THOMAS NELSON
& ZONDERVAN

WestBow Press books may be ordered through booksellers or by contacting:

WestBow Press
A Division of Thomas Nelson & Zondervan
1663 Liberty Drive
Bloomington, IN 47403
www.westbowpress.com
1 (866) 928-1240

ISBN: 978-1-9736-5656-2 (sc)
ISBN: 978-1-9736-5657-9 (e)

Print information available on the last page.

WestBow Press rev. date: 03/06/2018

Dedicated to the life and memory of Clenton Ray Chancellor.

My journey with him and without him.

Contents

I was cleaning out a closet to make room for my new husband's things and I noticed an old briefcase in the back of the closet. It didn't look familiar. I carried it to the living room and opened it with excitement. It was filled with hand written yellowing pieces of paper. The handwriting belonged to my late husband. I believe his poetry and drawings were meant to be shared with the world. Some were written during his high school years as well as after he met me.

Clenton and I self-published a book of poetry in December 2004 titled More Than Words: An Emotional Journey. His health was very fragile and painful in 2002 and the following year. He wanted to leave some sort of legacy. I saw an ad for Author House publishing. Clenton agreed that his writing could not only touch the lives of his family but inspire strangers. We saved for the cheapest publishing packet. Getting published resulted in a local newspaper interview but it didn't make us rich in money. The newspaper article gave us our five minutes of fame.

God gifted me another 7 years with Clenton. Those years were rough years for him, but he never complained. He often said that 'if my suffering inspires one person to appreciate their life, then my suffering was worth it." 2011 was a sorrowful year. February, we said goodbye to his oldest brother. We attended his funeral. Clenton stood looking at his brother in the casket and said, "please don't place me in a box" My response was I promise but we have a long time before we cross that bridge.

July 12, 2011, I had gotten dressed for work. I walked to the door to leave but I decided to check on him one more time before leaving. He turned towards me with a grimace on his face and said, "how did you know my chest was hurting." I went into caregiver mode, getting him dressed within 5 minutes. I drove faster than I ever had. The hospital admitted us and yes, I mean us. I was always by his side. My life was his life. The doctor scheduled his for a cardiac test in the morning. I slept in a chair next to his hospital bed, well I didn't sleep. I listened to his breathing. He looked so peaceful. He was smiling while sleeping. Morning arrived, and escort personnel took him to his test. I went downstairs to the cafeteria to eat breakfast. I had just returned when they wheeled him into his room. Immediately I knew something was wrong. The escort said, "he hasn't responded to me" My response to her was; and you just wheeled him back here with telling anyone. I looked at his glassy eyes and told him I loved him. He whispered, "I love you." I placed in bed and he became flaccid and non-responsive. I pulled to call light, and no one came. I went into the hall asking for help. I was told his nurse wasn't available. I returned to his bedside and I knew this was out last visit to this hospital. The attending doctor came into the room. He said he had a seizure and I said he hasn't had a seizure he has had a stroke; can we get a ct scan?

I got on the phone and called our best male friend and told him. I felt that Clenton had a massive stroke and would he come to the hospital. The neurosurgery team came into the room as they wheeled Clenton back to his room. I was told by the doctors it was a catastrophic event and I had minutes to decide if I wanted them to do heroic surgery which would leave him as a vegetable or let him go peacefully. I let him go. I called my job, my family. I called one of his family members and was told "we are running errands, we will come up when we are done" I guess we had been in the hospital so many times that they didn't think it was urgent. I sat on his hospital bed watching his labored breathing. Someone touched me on the shoulder. My coworkers, church family, my family had filled the room unnoticed. The air was filled with sympathy. I walked out of the room just to keep from crying. I had to be the strong one.

He was placed on hospice and they hung an IV with pain meds in it. Everyone had gone by 630pm. I leaned to kiss him as a tear rolled down his cheek. I whispered I will be okay, you can go now, I love you forever. His arm raised up as if trying to hug me and then he was gone. Clenton R Chancellor born October 7, 1963 went home July 13, 2011. I kept thinking what am I going to do? My soulmate of 23 years is no longer suffering but I am alone.

This is a picture of Clenton wearing his favorite hat looking up to heaven. His relationship with God and Jesus was first. He was truly an inspiration to all who knew him. The writings he left behind were from his youth before he and I met as well as the beginning of our journey together. The following pages are filled with expression of love, life, death, grief and redemption penned by Clenton as well as me.

Being Together

I call her name by and by,
Then we're together again…
Just her and I
With love so grand we hardly care
About the world around us or anywhere
We're together, our hearts are the same
Two mature lovers, not playing a game
No living without her
It wouldn't be right
Like the moon and stars not shining at night
She caresses my chest sighing with awe
And dreams of a night I never saw
We kiss in the dark
Committing no sins.
Nature is upon us and the cycle begins.

Memory

Memory is a gift
We walk along hand in hand
Just her and I upon the land
Our words were spoken eye to eye,
With one sweet kiss under the sky
"hold us strong please heaven above
And keep us together in a tight
Bond of love"
We're in love and the world doesn't matter
Cuz when we're apart it never seems sadder
I hold her tight and look into her eyes
Share something special and skip the surprise
Infinite love and total desire,
One for the other, both are in dire
We stopped along the flowers and lay
And look at the stars with nothing to say
Soft and easy the love of ours,
The feeling is strong
And gives us the powers.

Just

Just when I wanted to argue again,
Just when I wanted to fight,
You look at me
With those crystal eyes
And the moment melted right
First when I thought
I was giving up, you held my hand and understood
Just a moment till the sun
Ever is lost this dawning
Thus, the day begun
A teardrop fell into the sea
Swallowed into time,
Just one remembers it
A teasing echoed memory
Something that was would never be
A teasing memory
Just one remembered it
Teardrop swallowed by the sea.

WAR

It is death and pain
Milked and strained by right and wrong
But it's war
Its time is indefinite and lonely and long
Each hour of sleep is racked with guilt of every life I took of every fort
we built
The need of peace weakens my soul
Every breath gets harder as I crawl through this hole
The meaning of raunchy reeks a stench through the air
Be it death or the dying it isn't fair
Either north or south, the blue or gray
They all cry when they die the very same way
Alone I stand against the chance
Of death and sadness and their poison lance

Words of Wisdom

Love is pleasant and always there,
But if the time isn't right you never care
If innocence lies in the purest best
Then the time for love belongs to the rest
If love is fire and time is in the wind
The seconds pass, and our hearts never mend
To find a heart that beats the same
You love someone and play the game
Add the good and minus the bad
Love's little answer is sometimes sad
Before the sun begins to rise
The love inside is no surprise
Your heart will burn if it isn't gold
If it's pure its young it will never grow old
The story of love is written in the eyes
The window of wisdom where the heart never lies.

The Pain of Desire

Once twice a thousand times
We've felt the heat of the fire
It burned us once and then again
You can't escape desire
Our spirits try to deceive the truth
And try to hide a lie
But the nirvana always reflects you
And we cannot reason why
Love is desire, desire is pain
And maybe in lonely darkness
The answer lies in vain
Be it a gift or be it a curse
We never find our way
How can we find the answer?
Somebody needs to pay
Where does the answer lay?
As the rigid fingers of pain
Takes the love away

The Room

My room is perfect for a seance because it's dark and silent except for the noises I hear

Coming from the closet but that's a different story. I was looking around the house comparing rooms for my seance then I discovered my back room would be perfect. I set up a black candle, lit it and sat down beside it, around fifteen minutes afterwards I started feeling dizzy and, in my mind, I flew through a tunnel. The tunnels seemed to go on forever and as I flew I saw lights that looked like sparkling diamonds.

Ride

Take a lonely ride
Find out what's inside
Dream all your cares away
I tell him my troubles
Tell me what's wrong
I still feel lonely
But I'm taking the ride
My life has changed
A willing partaker
I miss sometimes
So, I dream them back
I take the lonely ride
In spirit I, not here
Cause I'm dreaming in fear of loneliness near
I tell him I'm troubled, but will he hear
Sometimes it's a question will I come back?

Untitled

Gone tomorrow and here today if
Love is eternal it'll never sway
Eye to eye and heart to heart love
I will tear your emotions apart
I gave you poems, can go on for days
And those are my ways
I end this poem with my point of view
Love is grand and ill share it with you

The Pills

I almost lost my life last night
In suicide but now I'm all right
I took some pills to make me sleep
And never wake up my soul to keep
I woke up the next morning and watched the sunrise
And those beautiful trees and birds in the skies
I've never known what life means to me
Thank God for life, life and the eyes to see
Just today, I gave someone breath with a breath of hope
When she was close to death.
Now that I know what it means to die
I can feel for others and maybe need a cry
Once a heart begins to beat
It deserves the strength to face the heat
If every eye could see the way
That I see the world every day
Take this advice that I give to you
Most sentimental moments in whatever you do.

Untitled

A magic place where lovers meet
A fantasy world called the lovers retreat
Secret moments are often the minute you're there
And you never leave lonely, only a pair
You savor the moments when you hold them close
And all that is needed is one gentle dose
You laugh, and you sing like lovers always do
When your heart is in trouble
There's someone new
It's all in your mind this wonderful place.
I'll leave you in pain without even a trace
That way your heart may be lonely, but you'll find her someday.

Untitled

One touch of your hand
And I smile
As the days go by the memories make
One touch if your lips
My heart's caressed
Puts the beauty back in life
Come how I think we're blessed
One hug as I hold you tight
Makes everything alright
It carries me through the bad
Builds my dream at night
Yes dear, you got my love
And all I got is yours
First carry it through time.

Car

I started my car and wondered if it was really getting up early every Saturday just to get a good deal at the flea market. But that's what my life has always been like, garage sales and bargains. My dad and I always had a knack for talking the price down to at least a third off. He died last year leaving me two oddly painted aluminum cubes, he kept them always in a small marble box inside his closet door which was thick and hollow. Ever since he was a little boy, he would take them out and shine them brightly because his great grand mother gave them to him and he felt honored to have them. On her last dying day she told him that there was another cube that was lost down through the ages.

Clenton and I went to Walmart and bought red spray paint and spent a morning painting his old truck which had a hole in the floor. I remember getting stranded between Temple and Killeen

Spring has come and opened our eyes to the ways of the world and those of the wise

The flowers are showing their color all satin and green
And the fields hold nature soft and serene
Among the blades of grass and hay
Between the trees where chipmunks play
My mate and I found our place
Just under the sky slowing our pace
Nature's gifts are there to see
Just her and I consistently
We cherish the things nature will share
Like the things we saw when man wasn't there
We earned the moments that nature gave
Their memory of nature goes into my grave

Love comes with tears
And tears come with pain
And you can't have sunshine
Without any rain
Love comes with bliss
And bliss comes with time
And you can't find a heartache
Without finding a crime
Love comes with memories
To treasure and to keep
But memories are priceless
And never come cheap
Love comes with dreams
And dreams come with hope
Hope comes with faith
For without faith we can't cope
Love comes with softness
That always turns rough
And happiness is scarce
There is never enough
Love comes with reality
Hidden behind dreams
Forever in sweetness

Never sleep or
The dreams will come
For a wishful dream
Of love will tear
The many lonely seam, a tearful love
Is whispering call; is do first lonely song
To hollow darkness fall, teardrops after

Heartache in a sea of violent pain
Unanswered are the questions
Where confusion remains
This lonely heart remembers
A day of love's caress
Which love sparks of hope
That once was aide to rest.

Tell Them the things they need to hear
Show them all your love no need to fear
Alone at night just follow your needs
Your need will match up just follow the leads

Love is laughter togetherness all
Love is fine just wait and see
Find a love and set your soul free
Goodness gracious burning desire
One night in love can you feel the fire
Its hold and cold and always there
Just let it loose, it's not even fair
They'll catch your eye you lose control
Burn the night feel loves soul
Catch a dream and let it fly
One night in love under one starry sky
Your heart will beat the same as theirs
Be yourself don't put on airs
Love is a song, song within self
Set love free not on a shelf

Love is sunrise let it shine
You'll both be happy let's build a shrine

A magical moment to have and share
Holding her close these times are rare
The energy flows from soul to soul
Its love and it's there and never grow old
Find the time to look in the eyes
The seconds do pass like unwilling surprise
Memories come they make you cry
Remember the times spent under the sky
You laugh, and you smile during that time you had
And when the memories passed it will make you sad
My advice to your young people I know
Appreciate times before they go
I write the poems up I'm able to see
Sentiment's blind whenever you're free
I've seen the world I know what I say
I've been through the pain don't let yourself stray
My heart is older than those I've known
As I teach the young heart isn't shown

Eternal love a promise I give for romantic sentiment is all I should live

Let's come together and glue our hearts, and beat together as one if it starts

Let's hold hands and enjoy it I say

Give me a chance I'll never stray

If I could cap the bottle of time

I'd stop it for good and spend with the very last time.

My feelings have spread on paper for you

If your answer is yes, you'll never be blue

Maybe I've said a little too much

But my heart is beating, and I need your touch

My Life My Love

Graced into my memory
And tended with the best of care
These precious times remembered
Held and locked in my heart somewhere
Fast is time when I share my thirst for love
The future unfolds the past
Guides the present oh that gold laden past
A treasure chest of love
Besides mishaps, the tears, I had memories
Our family built strong designed to grow
Even stronger in a home secured forever
A warmth that's sure to please
Make the importance of my life
Every piece of every thought pf them
Molded me to be me

Karen

Love is pleasant and always there but if the time isn't right you never care. If innocence lies in the purest best, the time for love belongs to the rest. Time is going into waves of past take your time and let it last. If love is fire and time is the wind the seconds pass, and our hearts never mend. So, find a heart that beats the same, love and play the game. Add the good and minus the bad, love will sometimes leave you sad, Before the sun begins to rise, the love inside is no surprise. Love is great if you know how to play, just tell your feelings if you know what to say. Your heart will burn if it isn't gold and if your heart is pure it'll never grow old. The story of love is written in the eyes. If love is strong it never denies but first let's talk a while, to find ourselves behind the smile. We've known the times together but blind. Our childhood is gone, let's leave it behind. I see someone new when I look your way, a love like yours I'll never betray. Let's set our soul for permanent bliss and leave for paradise on just one sweet kiss. Karen, I think the time is now, our lives go on, but it isn't wow! My thoughts are honest at least they are shed.

Dear lonely heart your time has come,
To find your place among the glum
You're set in your ways
And in time you will learn
A truer heart will never burn
You've had your turn
And now it's theirs
Just study and watch the numerous pairs
You've had your flowers
In your time
But wanting someone is not a crime.
You think back in times
Of your happiest best
From memories of glory
And those you were blessed
Your heart aching
But you take it in stride
You're fighting a battle
But your hands were tied
Well time has passed just fade away
Keep on searching you'll find her one day.

It's a ride of beauty and a ride of pain. It has taken me through happiness and hurt. I'm still on the ride but it's hard to sit still. I've felt a lot of eyes and a lot of hearts. I've kissed a lot of lips and held a lot of hands. I felt a lot of pain and touched a lot of hearts. I've been through hell and lingered in heaven. I've loved and lost, cared and won. I've been the lonely and was the man. I've felt fire. I've felt rain. I've felt hurt and pain but baby it's time to find love.

SOME DAY
THIS WILL BE
REAL

Clenton and I would hide love notes all over our apartment as well as a house. I found these after his death.

I love
you too,

and thanks for

being there.

P.S. It will
always be an honor
for me to be your
husband.

"HI, It's me again. I'm just writing to you because I couldn't tell you over the phone, plainly… I miss you through all my creative inspirations and dire inclinations. I could not find any other word that could measure up or say with such exactness as those three words. I as a writer and thinker couldn't replace or change the precision of an old-fashioned phrase but who needs to, anyway I miss you. I could however decorate this phrase with prose."

I Miss You
Every time I turn around
No matter where I go
With each hour
I think of you, ya know
Our time of love was brief,
That I hope continues
Your arms around me I need again
Cuz to you I'll be ever drawn

That was not one of my best, but it delivers my point I am now the happiest man in the world. I may not, be a good talker but be patient with me and my word will turn into voice. Now, in this package is something I hope you will like. It is kind of special to me because of the way I found it.

Amongst a million and half stuffed animals of which I dug through in 2 hours, there was this little guy. I don't know what made me notice this one but when I did he looked up at me with the saddest eyes. I picked him up and there stuck to him was a doily. After I got home, cleaned it and ironed the doily his eyes kind of smiled at me. If he had a mouth it would have a smile from ear to ear. He looks dashing sitting amongst the flowers it came with. So, I hope you remember this little history and take good care of him, give him a name and remember me Love Clenton

Shyness

Come to me shy one
And be my friend
For the time is nigh for happiness
And loneliness to end
Discover me and my world and see
The wonder of this life
Uncover what is hidden now
Let loose your stress and strife
Let me see you and your world
Let me find what is inside
Show me what's you girl
Relax and open wide
Time will tell if we spend it
As destiny unfolds its secrets
But unless we use them wisely
Regrets will follow yet.

Smile of Sudden Peace

Somewhere in the world, the cold cold world amidst the hatred rescue me, cold and bitter dream of cold and bitter days. In a life of unattained pain, the heart plays along this old forgotten man still believes his faith in love is strong, the sun may rise tomorrow, life goes on today, no stopping him from waiting for love to come his way, his past was lain roughly. His heart broken used and sad, but he still believes that love will come better than he has ever had. One morning the sun did rise and pushed the lonely moon away and he found himself in cupid's route in a park of hope's display. She was just happy by him, in a chance encounter they met, their lives would change forever. He saw her and within her smile suddenly bliss. She rescued him from a lonely life. With love and every kiss, the lonely moon is further away.

Darlin, my darlin sweet baby of mine just a card or a few lines to say I'm glad you are my valentine I'll love you in the morning even more midday and keep loving you at night Cuz baby I love your way so just to say I love you on this card I planned tonight and wish you Happy Valentines and hope it turned out right Love Clenton

Darlin when you smile at me it fills me with happiness, gives me strength. Me without you, angel I am weak, I love you through and through for as long as you can stand me, the pounds you gain are the pounds I love no regret nor shame when you]re by my side hand in hand we walk and eye to eye we face the world.

Our marriage was blessed with such sweetness and love. Clenton made real sacrifices for me as I did the same for him. I remember he saw this 4 -wheeled cycle. He fell in love with it. He rode that this as often as he could. I was missing my best friend who live in Springfield, Missouri but didn't have enough money for two plane tickets. Clenton offered to sell his 3- wheeled and 4- wheeled cycles to raise the money. I told him I couldn't let him give up something that brought him such joy. He replied, "making you happy is my joy". Clenton was one of the most giving souls I know.

Clenton loved animals and had wanted to be a veterinary doctor. I witnessed him take a baby rabbit our dogs had tortured and nursed it back to health. He would carry it in his shirt pocket to keep it warm. Clenton fed it with a syringe. I told him that a wild animal belonged in the wild. His responded "Beep-beep doesn't know the wild. I thought, oh no he named it, I guess we have another pet.

The rabbit grew to the size of his hand. He decided it would be happier with other rabbits. We drove to an overgrown grassy area and placed BB in the grass. Clenton cried as he stood there watching until BB was no longer visible. Every time we drove by the area Clenton would look over and say, "I hope he is doing okay, I wonder if he misses me". I finally caved in and stopped. I wish I had camera. Clenton made some squeal noises and moments later BB hurried out the bushes into Clenton's hands. Two weeks after we brought him home, he ate some rat poison and passed away. We had a nice funeral for BB as we did for every pet of ours that passed away. Clenton and I were parents to a baby bob cat, parakeet, cats and numerous dogs. Some got stolen, some wondered off and some died. I currently have our 13-year-old long- haired dachshund named Snookey B. He imprinted on me after Clenton passed. I think about getting another dog, but it wouldn't be fair to my very protective Snookey. Cancer took Ember and Teddy two years apart.

Teddy is the big dog. Next to him is Ember and his number one buddy Snookey. Clenton and I would lay snuggled with the dogs in a full bed. It was the most peaceful sleep I have ever had. I long for those days.

The moment I met Clenton I knew he and I would be a family. I could sense him when he was near. My heart and soul loved him after three weeks of dating then he put the brakes our relationship. I wrote him letters confessing my true love to him. He didn't respond. I wrote his sister Beth a letter telling her how much I missed him and loved him Three days later he was outside my apartment giving his dog Misty a bath. I ran into his arms. We stood holding each other. He said "the reason I backed away was that you're changing me in a good way and it frightened me. My response was, I simply love you.

I am unsure when leaving little notes and love poems began but here are a few I wrote to him, which I found in the briefcase with his writings. He was the true. I just floated along tailwind. Clenton taught me what real love meant as well was what it meant to give from the heart. He and I celebrated birthdays together. I was born one day and one year later that Clenton. We decorated our home for every holiday, but Christmas was our favorite. This a picture of our first Christmas in our house. I remember our last Christmas was spent in a hospital setting. That year we didn't exchange gifts and we had burgers for our meal. It was about just being together.

My Darling Clenton
My darling I love you.
You have made my life,
Filled with bright warm sunshine
Mysterious soothing moonlight.
Our love for one another will be
Always greatly tested.
If our destiny is to share our lives
And love together will withstand
The scorn and hatred.
My darling Clenton as each day
Goes by my love for you grows deeper and stronger.
If some day we must part, I will look back lovingly.
At each precious moment we shared together.

My heart will always remember "us" in a loving way.

My End?

don't grieve for me,
don't be sad,
rest has stopped the life i had.
i was ready, tired as i was,
worked had so long to further the cause.
i love some of you all here today.
and love is eternal, just put away.
miss me in memory and i will be there,
the times so precious, i am everywhere. . .
look up there in the clouds --- i am up there with Him,
trading jokes, laughing at whim.
i will be behind the smiles, chuckles and heart,
when time remembers my lifetime's art.
turn the page, go on stronger because you knew me,
and in the lap of God i will be.

by Clenton

Untitled

I love you so very much
That sometimes it frightens me
Sometimes I wonder if this is just a wonderful dream
And I'll wake up standing alone.
A lot of people give us dirty looks
A lot of people don't want us together.
Some don't think our relationship will last.
I know my heart's desire; our love will be everlasting.

Just A Note

Lying here on the sofa
Watching the wind gently blow the leaves on the tree
Hearing the song birds outside my window.

I realized how much I love you, I cannot see myself without you. Every time a car passes by, my heart starts to pound in hopes that it is you.

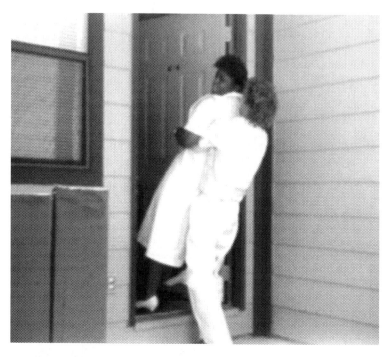

We said good bye our 23rd year. Memorial service Northside Church of Christ, Temple TX

Memories of moments are good to keep safely packed away in a special place. I said till death do us part in the spring of 1988 and death parted us in summer of 2011. Grief is a strange but individualized noun.

The day after Clenton's death. I got up early as usual. I called his name without hesitation. I realized the evening happened and he was no longer on this earth. I told myself no more tears. I drove to Wal-Mart and walked to the card section looking for Thank You cards. I bought one for each doctor that was kind to us during to 10 years of Clenton's health issues. I hand delivered one of the cards to our primary doctor. When I saw him behind the desk I started crying? The staff walked me back to an exam room. He asked me "what is with you today" and I staring at a wall replied I guess the hospital didn't notify you, we lost him last night, what am I going to do next. Everyone that knew Clenton loved him. All that loved him mourned his passing in their own way. I wrote down my feelings.

Some Days

Some days I see a butterfly. Some days I feel a soft kiss on my cheek. Some days I can almost hear you call my name. My life will never be the same. I spread your ashes near your favorite place to be. Every morning I rush to the window to watch the sunrise. I close my eyes and make a wish on the sun's rays. I open my eyes only to find out you are still gone and the ache in my heart is still reality. I have noticed on the days I am most troubled a red cardinal appears in the crepe myrtle tree or chain link fence outside our bedroom window. I immediately say hello and the loneliness lessens until the gift flies away.

My heart is a prison of grief's embrace. When night arrives, I close my eyes and think to smile through the pain. I turn off the noises in our house hoping to hear echoes of your laughter. My heart breaks in the silence of loneliness.

The memorial was very emotional. So many people admired your stoic attitude. I asked everyone to wear red with blue jeans. We celebrated the life of a beautifully inspirational soul. Our friends and family got up and spoke such kind words about you. I did not doubt you loved each person that attended your home-going.

I sat listening to James McNeal (recorded) singing Amazing Grace trying to remember the last few we had. Once you said, if you were granted one wish, you would wish for a new body, so you could have more time with me and the second one you looked at me and said, "I did not know what all you have done but I forgive you because I love you." Clenton how will I survive this world without you. You are the only person that has allowed me to be me. We both were free spirits intertwined who dreamed of changing the world in positive ways. You changed my life the moment you smiled at me the first day we met. I feel cheated. My heart longs for just one more moment but one moment wouldn't be enough.

I was dreaming of a moment in time. You were standing close enough to touch. My heartbeat was in sync with yours for a moment. there was only one slow lonely beat. My eyes opened from slumber. My heart was calling your name. I realized that you are no longer physically present. WE shall never be the same. The moment you died, my essence died, and my strength transformed into weakness.

Thunder

The sound of my falling tears is like a silent thunderstorm.

How will my soul face the next second without you?

Will another love me unconditionally?

My heart breaks in a million pieces every time your memory enters my dreams

Someone to me to get over your passing.

I doubt they know what it feels like to lose part of your soul.

Time doesn't heal this deep longing, just one more moment, I wish for

Although one more moment is never enough.

I see smiling faces my ears hear laughter

The sun shines in bright blue skies

Yet silent thunderstorms fall from my eyes.

I lay awake remembering memories faded and clear

I stand in the wind hoping to hear a whispered "I love you'

I feel a soft imaginary caress on my cheek.

My heart will always be in pieces, it may love again but not the same

Silent thunderstorms fall from my eyes forever.

Many may not understand or agree with my grief

May not agree with my choices to comfort the loneliness

I don't care. This is my journey not theirs and not yours

Grief is an individual deeply personal journey.

8-10-11

I feel so lost at times
I miss you so very much
Snookey looks at me and whimpers
I hold him and my heart weeps
I try to comfort him, but I am not you
I look around the room searching for something that would tell me
this is a bad dream

If only you were standing in front of me smiling about to tell me one of
your silly jokes; I can almost hear your laughter. I look at your photographs
and I feel loved unconditionally but now alone I miss you.

I remember how you and I rarely missed the setting sun. We both felt that watching the day come to an end was beautiful like a poem.

The sunset is more beautiful
When thoughts of you flood my mind
I was looking forward to sitting on
Our bench on Fall evenings watching
The days come to an end
And now I sit alone
With lonely cold tears
There is a breeze strong enough
To make the leaves dance around
The chimes are playing our melody
Can you hear it in heaven? Are the other angels singing?
Hold a spot for me. I will be there one day

2018

You know what kind of journey I have had since July 2011. My health is a wicked enemy, but I am blessed. My mind tells me I will be back to work soon, but my body says, "girl please." I stopped answering the phone. I say to the bill collectors I will pay once I return to work or get disability. I still want to work, but the reality is that I should retire. I should have retired when I went into left -sided heart failure. I had to return my retirement vehicle. My entire body hurts all the time. I have been hospitalized numerous times and missed a great deal of work. My eyesight is fragile. April, I had surgery on both feet after eye surgery the previous month and in May I had the second phase of the foot surgery. I had made a Go Fund Me page and a Facebook fundraiser. I had three people donate. I had a few people apologize for not donating, had a few tell me their troubles and I even had someone send me a link to a charity they donated to. I had a good friend tell me I could ask him for anything except money. I guess most people have troubles of their own and need help themselves. I took the pages down. My bills are delinquent A few members from the church has been helping with rides to my doctor appointments and they helped with meals for a couple of weeks. Their assistance is a blessing. I was on the prayer list for a week. I don't ask anyone for money or even food. My family helps as much as they can. Worry stays on my mind. I don't sleep much. I feel like a failure at saving enough money that would last a year. The house needs so much work don't to it, I know God has a plan for me. I lean on my faith which needs a recharge. My spirit is tired but whenever I want to lay down and die, I think about what you often said if my suffering inspires one person in a positive way then it was worth it. I have started writing again. I believe it was meant to emerge during this part of my journey.

Standing at a fork on the road
During my journey
My mind filled with constipated thoughts
I push and push the thoughts just won't pass
Thoughts of fragrant roses with pricking thorns
In the distance a soft lullaby
But a loud incoherent melody
I cannot stand here in limbo
Why can I not find the elusive unknown answer on this confusing road?

It has been 91 days since the first phase of my surgery on the right foot and 109 days approximately since my right eye surgery, I am lucky I haven't been fired a long time ago. I need a miracle. I have no money to even buy a sno-cone. I am sitting here thinking about all the things I need to buy or want to purchase. I have so many delinquent obligations it's making my heard hurt. My heart is pounding so hard. I don't know how I will ever get out of this debt. I hope the bank can sell the vehicle for what I owe on it. I no longer answer my phone. I sound like a recorded message "Yes this is her speaking, no my situation has not changed. I did not have any other resources. I have stopped asking anyone for funds. I could use 20 bucks. I have been craving Chinese food and seafood. I would have to ask someone to go get it, because if I could drive I had to give my vehicle back. I pleaded my case to death ears. It was so much easier for me to get in and out of my SUV.

I imagine things are overwhelming for my new spouse. He is not used to being responsible for another person He is forced to pay all our mutual bills; my co payments and buy food while dealing with my poor health and a home that requires so many repairs. He works 8 hours in another city. The highway isn't an easy drive. He performs all the household chores including cleaning out my bedside commode that has been sitting all day. He loves me. I just want to be happy and peaceful for the remainder of my life. It takes money to have peace. I was raised to be independent and this not having an income is not something I would wish on anyone.

I get so lonely during the day. I have always found it strange that at the very beginning of a loss of loved one, an illness, a marriage one gets phone calls, food, visits and then people go back to their own lives. I am still trapped in this house until someone is kind enough to take me on an outing other than a doctor's appointment. I often lay in bed looking out my window day dreaming about all the places I would like to go during my day. Depression kicks in and I start to weep inside. I don't understand why I cannot catch a break. I have always been kind to others, I place others needs above mine and yet I have had a shitty three years except for my wedding day and our trip to Vegas. I started working on my relationship with God. I know all blessings come from him. I feel that something wonderful is about to happen for me. I wish to be as rich as Oprah, Ellen and Simon Cowell combined. I could pay off my family's bills and open a nice women's shelter. I would buy hubby his dream retirement car. My friends that have n steadfast would get a great gift. I would buy the news crew at channel 6 breakfast, lunch and dinner for 110 days. I love the news and this channel has been a comfort to me. I am not a soap opera fan. I watch world news until the local news comes on. I watch reruns of the Golden Girls, Kathy Lee and Hoda, Ellen, Dr Oz and I listen to music to stay out of that dark place of depression. The dark place can consume you and you will become no more. One must feel their existence has a positive purpose, fee living this life means something. I must be productive. It was a blessing for me to find Clenton's writings as well as mine. This time off was maybe meant to be. God gifted us the ability to write poetry. Gifts are meant to be shared,

Seriously I want to be rich in happiness and have enough money to help others, I would name the Clenton R. Chancellor Christian Center. It would be a place kids can play, do their homework, get a meal during the summer and weekends. A women's shelter, with full kitchen and laundry, outdoor relaxation area.

I am having cabin fever. I print out adult coloring book pages. I color. My friends gifted me several coloring books, crayons and pencils one Christmas. My Elrese recently purchased 120 coloring pencils and a battery powered pencil sharpener. I color for hours when I should be sleeping. I should start sketching and painting again, I find wonderful pictures online most are copyrighted. Tonight, I will sketch something to share in this book. I just must figure out how to scan it into the laptop. Elrese just came home with my most favorite fruit in the world, cherry plums and two new pillows for my bed. I hope I can sleep tonight after I do that sketch. I was gifted writing, not drawing, although I did have a water color painting of a house in my junior high school display case. It was one of many others' artworks.

July 13, 2018.

I didn't cry outwardly today but I missed the sunrise on purpose. I stayed in bed until it was time to stop feeling sorry for myself. My phone starts buzzing the moment I feel peaceful. I tell them the same thing I told them last week. One company is threatening although I sent them a small payment. Reluctantly I requested a hardship withdrawal from retirement fund which is almost nothing. I am paying all my delinquent accounts, so they know I am not an abuser. I would consider risking the use of my legs by going back to work to pay everyone off but that isn't happening. I have told them I will make payments once I have an income I get severely depressed. I have enough medications to close my eyes forever, but I am still here. The thread I am hanging onto is very thin. My head begins to hurt thinking about all them phone calls. My mind is flooded with everything I am responsible for including being an example of a good Christian woman with flaws. A great number of people sit on the pews every time the congregation gathers. They smile, sing, act like they love all unconditionally but on Monday pass a fellow Christian on the street who is down on his luck, afraid they will ask for money. And all they need is a smile to get them their lonely day. That is what I call a Sunday Pew Christian sitter the adjective selective selflessness does exist in their vocabulary. I wonder if those fancy pew sitters will get into heaven easier than I. My life has been filled with intermittent bad choices. The time of night when no one in the world is awake but me I wonder if I am cursed because I don't sit on the pews as often as some think I should. I was once the poster child for the definitions of selflessness until I got burned by someone I shouldn't have placed faith in. My advice to you, place your strongest faith in God.

July 17, 2018

My gut feeling that something good is about to happen to me remained intact after speaking to my boss over the phone. I was informed that the hospital director will not approve my request for leave without pay instead of absent without leave. I had used all my FMLA hours with my first two surgeries. I guess the next phone call will be "you're fired but your 20-year pin will be mailed to you." My heart would break even more. I have been a nurse since 1985. I wanted to leave the profession on my own terms. Memories are bittersweet. I think about all the times I worked while ill pushing through just, so my coworkers wouldn't have to do the job of two people. Nurses are selfless people. Tears are rolling from heart. I love taking care of our veterans and working with the crew in outpatient surgery. I must decide before its made for me. My body and spirit are exhausted from the chaos of my curse/illness. I am reminded how Clenton must have felt. Some nights his pain was so horrific he would pray for God to take him and then he would ask God to forgive him for asking. Clenton had the strength to endure his journey as I must find strength for my journey.

Our home still needs work.

Our church family built a wheelchair ramp.

I have reset my life goals. Goal number one is not to give up on living. My number two goal is to continue never to allow anything or anyone to strip me of my inner peace. Chaos surrounds me, health related, financially, career related and emotionally. Clenton was the strong one and he shared his strength with me. No matter what was happening we faced it together. We were connected 150%. The past is nice to visit but one can't reside there.

I remarried a nice guy who was hit with a great deal after we said, 'I do". We are hanging in there. Our relationship with God is priority. It must be for us to survive the chaos. We attend worship services together when I am up to it and he has gone a few times alone. Fellowship helps strengthen faith.

I think I would have gotten more donations regarding my fundraiser, if one o my friends had set it up by telling my story. I am sharing pieces of my journey through happiness, utter sorrow, happiness and life- changing illness.

I remember when Clenton got shocked on the job led to the discovery of his lung sarcoidosis. He was never the same after working so hard in that foundry. I believe that job killed him or part of him. He lost energy. The job laid him off. He tried to get social security. They denied him until he suffered a stroke. It was a fight to get assistance. Many agencies stated Clenton wasn't a child or elderly. He received a lift for our vehicle and many other services after a year phone calls and emails. I may have the same fate. It has been one life altering occurrence after another since April 2017 with 8.5-hour parotidectomy and a parathyroidectomy with benign findings. May 2017, I am walking across a parking lot unable to catch my breath. My cardiologist told I had left sided heart failure and acute kidney injury. Shortly after that hospital stay I had left-sided heart failure. I began having severe pain in my feet and legs. I developed an ulcer on my left big toe. Several months later I gouged out a nice chunk of my left foot and I had to receive skin grafts and stay off work. It heals but a toe on my right foot developed osteomyelitis, a few weeks later the left foot. I lost a toe. I was healing from the last foot surgery and recovering from a second vitrectomy. A simple twist of my right ankle twice in one week revealed Charcot disease. I. had surgery on both feet. It was a miserable couple week. May 2018 I. had the second phase to repair my dislocated bones. It is a long recovery time. It is the middle of July and I still have not stepped on it. My left foot is doing the same thing. I have been working since I was 15 years old. I am having cabin fever and I don't enjoy being dependent on someone who is not selfless. It has gotten better with prayer and time. My podiatrist told me that this could happen again.

My body decided it's time to retire. I am not old enough, but I do have 20 years with the government. I am facing another life- changing event. It's the chronic pain that has my attitude bent. I then think about Clenton with his severe pain and seizures. I can do this. Enough of pain and sorrow for the moment.

One afternoon, Clenton and I found ourselves both off work. He came over to my apartment. No, we weren't married yet. We were doing things and heard knocking at the door. I peeped through blinds and saw my sister's and mom's faces. Clenton's dog started barking but we were quiet as church mice. I heard my mom say to my sister Loretta. "I heard a dog and there is his red car There is somebody in there, but we will come back" We rapidly got dressed. Clenton said "Am I not supposed to be here" I stopped and thought, and said I am grown woman and you are grown. This is my apartment, but she is bringing me food and money. You better go. We both started laughing. Especially after he left they pulled up. My mom said "I see your boyfriend I aint raising no babies' My mom and I loved dolls and stuffed animals. I would give her my old ones after Clenton would bring home a new one for me. Mom but rest in peace but you did raise my babies, stuffing and all.

We weren't the only ones trying not to make noise in my apartment. Clenton and I were sitting on my bed talking about how our day went. The windows were closed, the air conditioning was off. The bedroom door was closed shut. The bedroom door slowly opened, we felt a slight cold breeze while looking at the curtains moving on a closed window. I asked Clenton to stay the night. He and I were wide awake the entire night just talking and laughing. Spirits were attracted to us. An incident occurred with Clenton in our new house a few days after we moved in. I was sitting in a chair in the living room when I saw an old naked man from the bathroom. I told Clenton about what I saw. He told that that old man ghost enjoyed being naked. We also would often hear muffled voices coming from the walls. I can hear odd noises when everything is turned off during the day if I am alone.

I was just thinking about sunsets. A sunset is so beautifully bittersweet. It represents the ending of something. This Libra woman dislike endings. It's like watching a great movie, and then it ends. A darkness moves in causing utter loneliness. That is how I feel about the ending oh my journey with Clenton. I walked around functioning on the surface while dead in darkness of sorrow.

Grief is an individual journey. I would drive pass our house thinking I forgot to two plain just a burger for Clenton's dinner and I would reach for my phone to call his number. Reality would come blowing like a 5-f tornado his voice say, "Hi this is Clenton, do you know what, you know when, bye" He would get a country twang when he spoke sometimes. The rest of the world was so cheated. I was abundantly blessed with the unconditional love of a brilliant, passionate and kind soul.

I would like to re-share the poems published in our first book. These are more relevant now than they were in 2004. It's as if he and I were preparing for this moment on our journey.

Clenton's Poetry 2004

Born, Live, Die, Done.

Now that I'm grown and past the childish wants and wonders.
I sit here in reflection of past mistakes and blunders.
Still I wonder of this I did right.
Did I make a difference? did I add light?
Who am I to judge what course I took?
Born, live, die, done the answer in a book?
So, to get to age 36 and find my body diseased and dying.
And I replay memories, miss the times and start crying.
Grief for a short past of loves and hates,
tears for the moments gone for good,
tears for the space where I once stood

Goodbye for Now (Mom)

Christmas day I held you last your
Loving arms await my arrival some tomorrow.
My breaking heart knowing from this
Earthly existence you soon would pass,
I could say I was cheated given only
40 years to know a lady who to me
Was the epitome of grace and class?
But blessed was I; from you I learned strength in face of sorrow
Today the tears falling from my eyes
Are of sadness and of gladness.
Sad because will miss you so,
Glad because I know, in heaven your
Loving arms await my arrival some tomorrow
With love and admiration, your son.

Last Day of Regrets

Love ushers in beginnings
Time changes all,
Advancing days surprise, us,
Challenges befall.
Where I to dream differently,
I couldn't change the past,
I must collide with the here and now,
And persevere at last.
My last failing attempt to remember,
What good have I left here,
Gifts left behind rendered lovingly,
As moments disappear....

I Was Right Here All Along
Hiding tears from me fear of some unknown,
You yearn a fantasy love for gifts I don't have to give
You were dancing elsewhere secretly, yet here I was to live,
Terminally miserable
Yet forcing more days
Invisible wants to meet dead ends, or solitary ways,
Spirit away in secret dreams,
Look for me in other men,
And know that I am gone,
Was blinded by my love, but I was right here all along.

K, Now What?

I was strong enough to push against the strain life threw my way,
I withstood it all; against the grain I survived the day
I was strong yet diminished by fate
Because dwindling time showed me sickly.
Life had lost its taste…
To live strong in bitter spite,
Against disease my weakened plight.
Better days ahead
Strong against the thread

So Lonely

We were so happy in love and so young, we started this
We laughed and played at living and loving.
Years rolled by and. we grabbed at bliss.
Hungry for life we rushed from the past
Carelessly frolicking youth squandered at last.
Now we struggle to stay the clock.
Time has more memories and value to block.
Pain, loneliness, despair, dread
Loves lost in our hearts and probably dead.
Hindsight, hurting, emotional war,
Wishing, wanting for more,
Powerful jolts-I miss her so much
I miss her laughter, her kiss, her touch.
Gone now are the days we were strong,
Erased by apathy, long since long gone….

Virtual Circumstance

A type written game interacting characters play,
Two yearning players tempted for a moment swept away
With words we danced and had romance,
Imaginably loved in virtual circumstance
In my mind a damsel fair and small,
With beauty graced my air
And I a strong healthy buck,
Stroked here skin so fair,
Never thinking beyond it,
No repercussions could follow
A momentary taste of bliss,
But not enough to swallow
I, a handsome and young man,
She a heart rendering blossom,
Did borrow a dream and share it
Gratifyingly awesome
Goodbye for now

I Hurt

Aching for what the past was
When I could just believe
That love was the only answer
And I didn't have to grieve
Pining for her the way she was back then
I am a wasted heart hurt once again
Empty and cold, bitter and old
Story ended everything told
Love of living has since been sold
Worry and pain diminished
Entrance of blind distaste,
Overwhelmed by indifference, despair embraced

Injured Brain–Healed Soul

Horrific violent memories refresh my childhood pain
Denied for years, they were erased to me,
But then a stroke just let me see,
But now I have Jesus….
The peace from God's protection…
His holy word mends my wounded soul,
Such powerful selection,
Hope, faith and prayer sway tomorrow,
My future days on a positive thread.
The past's scathing terrors gone
And life goes on instead

Jeanetta's Poetry

Tears

Sitting here devoid of another human soul,
Only company I have are salty reminders,
Running down my face.
Reminders of love once true but untrue.
Faded memories of superficial laughter
Streams of salty reminders of pain
Running down my face.
Cobweb memories of false softness,
Its lasting mark a bleeding heart.
Only tired redness in these sparkle-free eyes
Salty reminders running down my face.

Standing in the rain
Searching for the sun.
Dark skies all my heart sees.
No shelter but dying trees.
Standing in the rain
Searching for the sun
Raindrops piercing my flesh,
Lightening crushing my bones
Wind carry away my soul,
Oh, where is my sun
Still time to save me?
Memories standing in the rain.

Still searching for the sun

Leaving

I must leave you now
Before the darkness catches me.
I must find the light before hope meets its demise.
The storm is too close. I must leave find my soul shelter.
Don't mourn my departure
But rejoice in the time I was here
Understand my need to outrun the darkness
Remember the moment of laughter and never forget my tears
Goodbye for a brief eternity
Leaving to find my soul's shelter.

Last Breath of Air

It is so cold in here. I can't seem to catch my full breath.
Why is everyone standing around me. bed
I cannot focus clearly am I dreaming this nightmare
Now this light is so bright. I think I know I hear voices
Singing voices. Such a beautiful sound, almost peaceful. I can't catch
my breath because it has ceased to be.
I am flying towards tranquility.
I am disappearing into the clouds of another journey. I am gone.

Memories

Sitting here glancing at your picture.
Thinking about the memories that could have been,
Replaying events over and over in my mind.
Still no explanation of our end I can find.
Oh, the memories that could have been.
The romantic sunsets we talked about sharing never to be.
You have someone special but it's not me.
The memories that could have been.
Spoken promises of taking care of me.
Promises that will never be.
Tears fall for memories that are not at all.
Heart aching for joy and laughter
But for us there will be no happy
ever after.
Memories that could have been

Email Affair

I received an email from a friend.
It stated "the relationship' had to end.
As I read it, my heart started to cry
Because in my heart I don't want to say goodbye.
But I know "we" must for a while.
From time to time I will remember you and smile.
My knight. Someone I will never meet.
Someone whose words swept me off my feet.
Your last letter was kind and sweet
But not a surprise that something so hot,
Awakening and forbidden would meet demise.
I think of all the places we could have gone.
I think of all the places we had been, but then remember
There was only one place.
Our special place, I want you to know that it will always be there.
Our moments will always be there between the commas, semicolons,
Periods and exclamation points. My heart, the part that remains
In unreachable deleted files, remains yours for the rest of my journey
This started out as a rhyme, but words of truth free flow.
I only want you to have the life you choose.
I want you to be happy in your real back yard.
I can say that I love you enough to erase.
Although my heart is hurting, I am glad your hard drive is safe.
Farewell, my knight
In loving memory, your internet princess.

Falling

Silent tears fall from my broken heart
Memories that will not be in each treasurer.
Hope has taken a long holiday this year
Silent tears fall from my broken heart
Prayers no good, lack of faith holds me back.
Tears leave a bitter taste.
Why is trying such a waste?
Silent tears fall from my broken heart.

Struggle

My souls struggling to hold on,
In the middle of this ocean of pain.
My soul searching for a small beacon
Of light, that will Lead me to an unknown shore.
At times I feel as of my soul has met its
Demise, in this ocean of pain and sorrow.
At times I grasp every rock and branch,
That crosses my path false feeling of hope
Only for a moment.
The struggle returns searching for that
Elusive beacon of light, struggling to save
This lifeless soul caught in a sea of madness.

I was rereading the poems I included from our self-published book in 2004. If the audience wasn't told there are two authors, they would think one poet laid his or her thoughts down on paper. Clenton and I basically wrote about the same things growing up and throughout adulthood, during our marriage, our relationship with Jesus. He and I enjoyed the same TV shows, movies, times of the year, music, we put others before ourselves. We both had things happen to us as a child that could have destroyed us, but they made us strive to the better human. My health has gone south just as his did. I am in a wheelchair without my own vehicle. Memory loss entered our world as time passed limiting he walk-a-bout. He was frustrated as I am now. I completely understand his feelings of being caged with no way out.

God gifted us 23 years of matrimony. Our children were our nieces and nephews. The fur babies were many in number. There is one old fellow left. He follows me every time I move. He must see me, or he will whimper. Snookey gets depressed if I get hospitalized. I miss you when I am ill and my mommy too. I can imagine the ruckus you two are causing in Heaven, cracking jokes with the other angels. I really appreciate the cardinal and butterfly visits. They seem to arrive just when I need them the most. I know God is with me on this journey. He was with us throughout Clenton's illnesses and the angels were present during our final moments together. Clenton, God's compassionate love help give me strength to go into care giver mode while not losing my identity as your wife. A great number of couples don't survive taking care of a chronically ill spouse. I have seen the healthier, seek out a nursing home, other family members, divorce or they just simply leave closing the door behind them. I cannot say it totally has to do with how much love you have for your spouse or the vows you took, keeps you in a relationship until death do you part. Perseverance as true team members facing whatever comes your way.

I wish I had fought harder for pain relief for you. Many of our close friends called you very stoic. I remember an urgent care visit. Your pain was off the charts, nothing you were taking at home eased the pain. The staff were so rude to you and me. The nurse call bell went unanswered and I was still ignored at the front desk. Returning to your bedside I noticed you were smiling. I asked you how you felt. You replied, "don't worry everything will be okay, my guardian angel told me." You were glowing and then you said, "your guardian angel is standing behind you" A calm conquered the chaos. The emergency room visits were frequent and many in number. I remember them all but this one stands out.

I turned our back bedroom into an office. The two evergreen trees we planted have grown so big. I can see them from my office chair. I often stare at them and day dream about what was and what could have been. I spread some of your ashes between the trees. Elizabeth your niece joined me that day. She held my hand as we prayed, cried and said goodbye. The picture you and I took at the photo booth and Temple Mall hangs above my desk and the International Star Registry. I would like to find your star one day. way

Rest easy my love. Mack takes good care of me and Snookey. He is wonderful friend. I will miss him terribly when he moves back to Mississippi. Elrese takes good care of us too. I dislike when a season is over, and friends move away. I dreamt of moving more north, but God has placed me where he needs me the most. My adulthood has been filled with many struggles. I pray a great deal and my faith tell me that my life is going to improve soon. I fake friends too. They taught me a few lessons needed to learn. I try my best to love like Jesus loved although some people make it difficult. Especially those that said "if you need anything let me know" then they disappear.

I understand the bond between Snookey and Clenton. Snookey bonded with me the night Clenton died and during all my illnesses. He is never far away. My heart will break again when he comes goes to heaven but then all our fur babies will be reunited with their favorite human.

Snookey was always in Clenton's arms. He loved riding with him on his scooter and wheelchair.

I believe memory is life's way to store random pieces of ourselves and others. Writing this book reminded me of the beautiful love I shared with Clenton and our fur babies. It reminded which friends are true. I often question my strength in error. I have gone through a great deal, but others have experienced worst. We were blessed, and I continue to be blessed with valleys that make me appreciate the mountain tops

PHOTOGRAPHIC PIECES

Clenton and I playing the Santa Fe Depot

Clenton lived the latter half of his life with a goal to one day meet Jesus.

Clenton was such a comical soul. He would sing along with the characters in the musicals we viewed together. Our favorites were Flower Drum Song and West-side Story. He loved scaring me too. The scariest thing to me was when he recited the opening them to Tales from The Dark-side. He would laugh so hard when my eyes widened in fear. I really wasn't afraid, I just wanted to hear his laughter.

Most of our evenings together were spent looking through our small telescope imagining how our lives would be if we lived on the moon. Our dessert every evening was walking hand in hand down our road and sitting on the front porch reading lines from our poems or a sci-fi book and sometimes comic books. We spent quality time together. He and I played video games and chatting online. It was our time one on one which was the most important. I believe his faith in God kept him pushing through the later years.

Attitude and a sense of purpose gives one a reason to want to wake up in the morning. My purpose for 25 years was to love Clenton enough to stay with him until the very end of his life, to love his fur babies as if he were still present, to find his legacy and make a positive difference with it. I trust he will be happy about my plan

I am not looking to get rich, but I want to help feed 15 families the week of our birthdays which is only two months away. I must change that date to October 7,2018 to December 31st, 2018. Monetary goal of $2000, hard copy and downloads $1700 to the Love of Christ food bank and $300 to print hard copies.

I am still on the fence about trying to get a publisher to pay be to publish our book but that is a pipe dream. It would be fantastic to get 20 thousand donated in his name.

I know some people find poetry difficult to understand and boring. I will share how I became a nurse and if I hadn't been a nurse, I would have never met Clenton or my bff Deanna McNeal. I had graduated high school and did not want to work in the fast food industry. I tried to enlist into the Air-force but that was not meant to be.

A fellow Christian recommended I become a nurse and he just happened to be on a hospital board that had an in-house vocational nursing school. I had to walk to the school on testing day which made me late. God had my back, I could take the entrance testing and I got accepted. I graduated February 15, 1985. I love taking care of humans at their worst. It makes me be a better person. I had wanted to graduate high school and instantly land a writing job for Time magazine. My heart and passion belong to Texas. I have only worked in two hospitals as my nursing career ends. I would work until I was 80 if my body would have held up. I would love to go into politics on a local level only.

Writing remains my first passion. I don't know if I am good enough to ever win awards, but it sure makes me feel as if I have a purpose. I will be 55 years old this year. I have no biological children. I try to live my life without regrets, but I am not perfect. God has saved me from myself many times. I don't know how much longer He will give me, but I am trying my best to see Jesus at the end of my journey.

Some of you knew Clenton more than you know me. I have included just a small glimpse of myself for your reading pleasure or boredom.

08/07/2018

Post-operative appointment went well. I was able to bear weight on my right foot for x-rays. My left foot is stable, and I can now wear a regular shoe on it. I still must wear a boot on the right foot along with an ace wrap to alleviate pain when it swells. Everyone in the podiatry clinic is so kind and passionate about helping their patients. I provided Dr S with a cartoon of Fred Flintstone it made him laugh. Laughter is a good for the soul.

It must be in the triple digits today but then again Lois doesn't have air-conditioning in her vehicle. I would purchase a new car for her if I ever won the lottery and I would get her house fixed up for her and Lee. I would build a 1000 sq. foot additional for hobby room for Lee, garage and storage building. I would pay all of Mack's bills off as well as my sisters. I would help my friends that have been steadfast. I would buy Elrese his dream car and build us a larger home with his man cave included. He is evolving into a nurturing husband.

My second appointment today was with pulmonary/sleep clinic. Dr B always looks so sad in his eyes. He smiles but his eyes look sad to me, Today I gifted him one of the hardest coloring pages. He was very surprised. I told him, if he was having a bad day, just look at the picture and imagine hiking through the forest. He is a nice soul. I feel I can tell him anything and he would try his best to help me. He increased my Paxil and added an anti-anxiety medication. I believe my depression and anxiety have heightened due to my chronic illness es and not being able to earn my own money. The day I gave up my vehicle part of my soul died. My ford escape was my gift to myself for being a nurse for almost 35 yrs. It was my retirement vehicle. If it is God's will in 6 yrs. I shall obtain another one, an upgrade with lower payments.

I need to play the lotto to have enough money to repay all the kind people who have helped me without expecting anything return. I would have to ask people not to tell anyone where their good fortune came from. Today was a good day. I came home and placed my night gown and started coloring. Coloring relaxes me a little. A couple of days ago, some good friends sent me a care package filled with adult coloring books and the most beautiful lap quilt. Elrese had gifted me some new coloring pencils and new coloring books recently. It gives me an anxiety outlet. I have started sketching again and of course I have my writing.

Every morning that I wake and see my two feet with its toes curling under, I am blessed. God has blessed me with another sunrise. Thank you.

08/13/2018

I did not sleep last pm. I am sleepy. My plan tonight is to color until I fall asleep. Tomorrow is my first social security disability appointment Snookey made us chuckle yesterday. Elrese had made dinner but he laid his plate on the sofa while talking to me. I heard him say oh my goodness. Snookey ran into mt bedroom so fast, I saw a blur of fur, ha ha. He had taken Elrese's chicken and was running like the wind. He has never done that. He must have been hungry too. I couldn't allow him to eat it, he would have thrown it up, he growled at me as a snatched it from his mouth. Elrese nicknamed him The Beast

08/14/2018

I saw the psychologist the social security people wanted me to see. It was difficult for me to climb steps with a knee scooter for a 15-minute interview. How can you know what a person is going through after asking a scripted list of questions? He did acknowledge that I have a great deal going on with my health.

I felt extremely depressed after that meeting. I wrote my podiatry surgeon explaining how disability retirement worked. He said my primary doctor should fill out the paperwork. The crappy thing is that she told me that no one in that clinic was qualified or allowed to do anything with disability. I am cursed.

I don't know if the surgeon will help me. My foot swells every time I get out of bed. Its painful 24/7. I have no padding on my heels. I was struggling before all the foot surgeries. I know for a fact I cannot do all that walking and standing. My sciatic nerves don't allow me to sit long. I am miserable. I do not sleep longer than two hours each evening. I am so sleepy during day hours that it is best I don' t cook on the stove or oven. It is almost like I pass out. I drop whatever I am holding in my hands. It is scary. I did not imagine the end of my life would be like this. I have never been a jealous hearted soul, but I see all the people who have told me they wish they could help me, prospering. I was always a giver because it made me feel good to help someone smile. am in dire straits and being avoided like a leper colony. I have one coworker that sends me greeting cards every two weeks. My phone only rings due to my numerous delinquent charge accounts. Suicide would be an easy way out of this world, straight into a hellish existence. My life that last few years have been hell on earth. Despite that I feel I am blessed in other ways. I have a handful of trustworthy friends and my family does love me.

I am sitting gazing out the one window in my home office. This house doesn't have enough windows. I would love to open them all up and if I had screen doors they would be open. I love the fresh smell on a windy day. I can see the two ever green trees Clenton and I planted in 1989. They were dried and dying. We only paid one dollar for them. I tear up with each glance. Bittersweet. They will outlive us.

Today I am not watching any television. I am so sick of politics or this variety show. I am listening to 70's music on DTV. I love music, its poetry with a melody. Last night I listened to IHeart radio Elvis station. My favorite thing to do to relax is listening to silence and music. I enjoy sad songs when I feel happy and vice versa.

I suddenly feel forgotten and discarded. I send people letters and cards, but I rarely get one in return. I turned my phone off to charge it and I get sick of collections calling and not leaving messages. I was getting the Lord's supper, but it stopped and not one person has called to see if I needed it. I know I don't feel worthy of God's love at present. I don't attend worship services like I should. I guess the congregation must be familiar with me to ask me how I am doing? I appreciate the help with rides and the meals after my first surgery. Those two things have been a blessing. There have been weeks that Elrese and I could have used more help, but I can sense people are afraid I am going to ask for money. I had a fundraiser as I mentioned in a previous passage. I heard someone close to me mocking it. I took it down for that reason and the fact no one wants to give money to someone who should have it all together. They don't realize my financial, spiritual and physical health has been shattered into almost nonexistence. It's okay. I know everyone has something going on. I will be glad when I am back able to help others until that happens, we are doing the best we can on one income and two income pile of bills.

Forgive me but sometimes the depression sneaks in and evokes self-pity. I have been battling this depression more since after Clenton's death. I know my anxiety has gotten worst since I have been off work. I just worry about things I cannot change. I try my best to lay my burdens down for God to take care of. He never lets me hit rock bottom. I do get on my knees often as we all should. My goal is to see Jesus welcoming me into heaven. I need to stop thinking negative thoughts and only embrace the positive. Deep down I feel something wonderful is going to happen for me. I claim it, I believe it.

There comes a time in everyone's journey that we must sit still and wait for the whisper of what God is trying to tell us. We may not hear what we want to hear but He tells us what He needs us to know. The Lord's time may differ from our desired timing but continue to remain quiet in the stillness. I thought I had finished writing this book but every morning, I have something else to place on paper. The older I become the more I believe in strength in having faith. When our final sunset arrives wouldn't it be a tragedy if we hadn't believed in anything our whole lives.

I had a doctor tell me shortly after Clenton had passed, that there really wasn't a heaven or hell. He said once we are dead, that's the end. I told him that one must believe that life on earth is just a stepping stone to something more beautiful. Jesus didn't just die, the end. He never spoke of his beliefs in my presence again. I continue to pray for him. I know without a doubt I have several guardian angels waiting on my arrival through those pearly gates. I must live a life that is pleasing to God. I want to see Jesus, Clenton and my mommy.

I had a friend tell me that the reason I had such a hard time with that in my past lives I kept making the same choices and same mistakes. I don't believe in past lives, if that were true, I would have been a butterfly previously or a gecko. I believe that my troubles are meant to give others hope in facing their own problems.

I heard words that I had been told once before, but the words were like a high voltage shock. My diabetes has been under control for several months, hemoglobin A1C is 7. My weight has decreased. I thought I was headed down the correct track. The endocrinologist instructed me to stop taking the Invokana due to the fact it was affecting my Stage 3 renal disease. I let go of the worry I was expressing regarding my toes curling under. The damage is done but with some dietary adjustments maybe I will never have to go on dialysis or require a new kidney. Lord, I am listening.

My pharmacy sent me a text, letting me know my prescriptions were ready to be picked up. I am blessed that 3 or zero dollars but the other two total 79 dollars. I have ten dollars to my name. I had to borrow money from hubby to pay for doctor's office visit today and I owe my dentist 105.00. I am trying my best not to fall to pieces, but I am failing miserably. So many illnesses. Diabetes causes a great deal of trouble if uncontrolled. If only I had stood still when I was 25 years old. I would have wonderful eye sight, feeling in my legs and feet. I must walk straight now.

I received a handwritten letter in the mail today. I think I read it 5 times. It is such a rare thing. People are so quick to text, snap chat, face time etc.

August 19, 2018

Last night I was craving some sugar-free wafers, but I had taken my sleeping pill. I was sleepy until Elrese tried to take away my wafers. He said my eyes were closed but my mouth was open, and I wouldn't let go of the sweet treat. This morning I joked that I would have turned into a beast. I know eating when asleep is a choke hazard, but I wanted them wafers. I must have passed out after snacking because I forgot to place my c-pap on and I woke up with a red coloring pencil in my hand. My eyes popped open at midnight with those wafers on my mind. I had a peaceful three-hour sleep but then muscle spasms in my chest was on the menu until daylight. A long hot shower helped the spasms.

I remember the dress I wore on the first day of school to Vandiver Elementary School. I was a shy child until I knew I could trust you. It was a day I shall remember until the end of time. My mom had sent me to walk with one of the older kids in our neighborhood. The older girl had decided she would skip school that day and since my mom told me not to lose sight of her, I skipped class. The truancy officer saw us. I had on a baby blue dress with daisies and no shoes. The officer took us to school. My first-grade teacher hit my hand with a ruler and said some negative things.

I knew skipping school was wrong. I also knew the color of our world growing up. Initially I spent my academic life proving her words wrong but, in the end, I had something to prove to myself. My opinion was the most important, if I were going to be a positive force in this world. I fell in love with school so deeply that I rarely missed a day after the first grade. My younger siblings caught the chickenpox and I did too. I was sixteen sitting in class with chickenpox. I was angry I had to be sent home. I made sure I didn't miss any homework. I was always three chapters ahead. I loved history and English. I am still terrible with numbers. I cant even pick the winning lottery numbers. Some anonymous person won 11 million this past week in Belton, TX I am happy for them, but I would be happier if they gifted me a blessing.

08/23/2018

It is going to be another day of 100-degree weather in Texas. The older I get the more I look forward to warmer weather. My younger bones loved cold weather except for one year in the 1990's. Clenton and I had gone to bed with a light blanket on our bed. I woke around 2 am shivering. The power was off, the water was frozen, and all the dogs were in our tiny bedroom. Clenton and I went around the house gathering everything we thought we could pile on the be to keep from freezing to death. Daylight arrived revealing the ugly truth, our power line was frozen solid, and I was unable to start our vehicles. Some friend drove into town to check on us and invite us to spend the duration of the cold snap at their house. We made sure the dogs had plenty of food, blankets, towels and our coats. I even covered the bird cage with a thick quilt.

I couldn't sleep worrying about our pets being cold and lonely. The next morning, the air warmed enough to thaw out our power line and we returned home to 4 happy dogs. I raced to the bird cage finding Mr. Bird had frozen and should have been named Mrs. Bird. She had laid an egg. I thought about becoming a bird owner late, but we decided it was best we didn't. and the house still doesn't get warm in the winter or cool enough in the summer. The 950 square foot space is still my dream home minus as additional 2000 square feet. I love this house like family. I want to have a gazebo built with a rose garden and fruit trees. A three-car garage and mega master suit would be nice.

The last few days I have been using a walker. My body hurts but I keep moving. I do not want to retire only to kick the bucket a month later I want to enjoy the fruits of my labor as healthy as I can be. I want to have stamps on my passport. A train trip across the USA would be a dream come true. I don't need a passport for stateside travel. Clenton use to tell me that "our own grass was green enough." I can only dream of traveling due to my poor health. My own grass is green enough but needs more flowers. Next spring, I plan to plant 25 rose bushes.

The past already happened, and the present is now, the future is neither promised or sure. Moments along our journey can randomly line into place without our consent. It is not the reaction that molds us but it our actions. I don't need to be famous or infamous. I want my actions to reflect something positive enough to help one soul. God sets His plans for me every time He opens my eyes. He sent Clenton into my life to teach me selfless love and believing in God enough to place that relationship in the top priority list. Clenton truly believer that his attitude towards his illness and constant love maxi dresses. I have lost weight since my foot surgeries; financially and body weight. Trying on the dresses made me feel beautiful. We can only afford one night away but creating memories doesn't have to cost a fortune Life is brief and fragile. Embrace the time God gifts you.

08/25/2018

I am sitting at my desk sipping on a sugar-free soda while writing a paragraph in the C and J legacy book. The excitement of visiting a historical hotel is making wish we were already there and able to spend the weekend. I will add this hotel to my bucket list.

08/26/2018

The Driskill is an elegant hotel located in downtown Austin. The lobby is warm and inviting. The hotel staff are very friendly and helpful. There is a rumor that the hotel being haunted. The only haunting I experienced was the aftermath of eating a huge Texas pecan waffle. It was covered with the largest berries and bananas I had ever seen. We hope to have better funding during our next visit to Austin. I am a homebody but traveling with Elrese is fun. I enjoy seeing other travelers on the highway.

My new motto is "Live, I deserve the best in life. Never settle."

The month of September was filled with doctor visits. My right foot is not healing well. The podiatrist ordered a bone simulator. It stays swollen and very painful. I decided not to return to work, well my body decided. I cried every night about not doing what I have done for over 30 years. I worry about losing my foot. The creditors call every day all day long. Some of them are very rude. I will be at peace once I get all those bills paid off because they don't understand circumstance can change without notice.

October 4, 2018

Today my coworkers gave me a 'Happy Retirement" party. I received my 20 yr. pin, hugs, roses and a beautiful cake and other nice gifts. I felt different at the end of the party. I couldn't say goodbye to anyone. I just quietly left the building. I know God places us where He needs us the most. I believe I was supposed to write this book, a legacy.

The employee lounge was yellow and purple. My cake was in the shape of a butterfly. There was a bouquet of a dozen yellow roses and two rose bushes. It was beautiful, and I felt loved. My sister and niece came up to see me receive my 20 yr pin. A couple of friends attended along with my work family. It was a bittersweet day. Something wonderful ended and something unknown began. It's almost like mourning a death of a constant part of your essence and you say "now what"

October 8 2018

I turned 54 yrs-old today. I don't feel older, but I am tired. Clenton's birthday was yesterday. I talked to him in silence. Only one friend on Facebook has donated to my food bank cause. No one seems interested in reading our legacy. Maybe if hard copies were available for sale more people would purchase the book. It just makes me sad. I really wanted to legacy to make a positive difference to something Clenton loved helping with while he was alive. I am not going to give up. Something amazing is just over the horizon. I think I will make a large donation with my own money. I guess everyone is having a financial slump or they don't trust me to give the money to the food bank. I don't know which hurts more, not helping to feed the hungry or not having the trust of people I've thought I knew.

October 16, 2018

I had my right foot x-rayed today. It revealed movement of one of the screws holding my bones in place. The pain wakes me up from the little sleep I get every night the surgeon instructed me to limit my activity, use ice and ibuprofen. I was so happy when I was told to bear weight on my right foot. Seeing the words "limit activity" is upsetting. Staying in bed all day or trying to maneuver a wheelchair in this small house is daunting.

October 18, 2018

I sat in the lobby next to where my spouse had come in to receive a flu shot. The employees were walking to the coffee shop locate in the same area. Envy filled my heart. I felt cheated. I loved working especially on the busiest days. It was never about making money to me. It was about making a difference in someone's life during their worst moment. I bumped into one of the nicest eye doctors I had the blessing to work with. I told her I was sad about having to stop working. She told me not to be sad because I earned this part of my journey. Smiling as she walked pass me, the she turned and said "enjoy the new."

I thought about those words most of the night. I felt hopeful and afraid. How can I not do something I have done for over 30 yrs.? My faith will give me the strength to face and conquer the unknown. God always sends comfort when I needed the most. I will survive on a fixed income. I will get all my bills paid. I will get a vehicle. I will enjoy the separation from a 33-year career in nursing. God is walking with me and on those days, I feel like crawling, He will carry me. It is true, with God all things are possible. We must remember He is in control of all blessings. The timing may not seem quick enough for us. God's timing is the best time.

October 23, 2018

Today I had planned on going into town to cast my midterm votes early. A friend drove to my house to give me a ride to the annex downtown Temple. We drove passed the full parking lots and the people lined up outside the annex. I will try again later in the week. More people are voting due to so much chaos in Washington, DC and America. The main reason why voting is important to me is the health-care in regard to pre-existing illness not being covered. There are a great number of people in America that are chronically ill including myself. My current insurance ends in a few days. I must stay out of the urgent care and doctor offices until January 01, 2019 unless I have enough money to pay cash for the visits. I am going to have to ration my medications. I need to win the Mega Million tonight. I could help so many people.

The state of our schools across America, the #me2, opiod crisis, gun control and racial divide are other reasons sending more people to the polls. I just pray that no fraudulence occurs with the ballots.

Today is October 30, 2018, It looks and feels like Spring outside. My rose bushes are blooming. It is a bittersweet day for our nation. 13 people were killed for being a different and practicing a different religion. There will always be hatred in this world but in 2018 it should lessen. Why can't everyone live under the same sky love as Jesus loves. Words spoken from the tongue are usually from the heart. Our current president disrespects the office he was elected to. He called a man running for governor of Florida as a Democrat; "a thief". I say "he who is without sin let them cast the first stone." I love America, but the current administration makes me want to wear a bag over my head. He tells untruths like he breaths oxygen. I don't know how the press secretary looks in the mirror after lying for him. I pray this administration doesn't screw things up too bad. I wish them success, but they do not deserve to do two terms. It's normal to disagree but not to the point of hating someone enough to think of ways to harm them. My faith in God gives me hope that our president realizes he should keep negativity out of the conversation. I still believe in humanity when the sun goes to sleep, the moon and stars dance across the sky. We all bleed red. We are all made of flesh. We all just want to be loved and feel safe while we live life.

October 31, 2018

A bowl filled with bags of m&ms, not one trick or treater knocked on our door, the container was almost emptied by me in 24 hours. Anxiety causes me to eat too many sweets. Retirement without money is so stressful but things will improve. I will have plenty of time to learn patience. I just realized I missed watching my favorite Halloween cartoon; "The great pumpkin" We watched it every year as children and I continued the tradition. Cartoons are relaxing. Laughter is better than shedding tears.

November 7, 2018

It has been a year since I first had pain in my feet and they still hurt. I can't feel my lower extremities sometimes and it's frightening. I often wake and immediately look to make sure I have two legs. Today I am using the wheelchair due to pain and fatigue. It is an overcast day, not because Texas remains a red state after midterm elections but because a cold front is passing through.

I love Texas. It is a great place to live. One needs transportation. I am so bored and feel as if I am in a cage without the key to open the door. My sanity is saved by writing this book. The TV has been off all day. I got sick of all the political hatefulness. I am more worried about the elected officials than the immigrants wanting a better life in America. It's depressing. It is time for some humor.

Clenton and I loved watching movies. One weekend he took me to Harker Heights to meet one of his sisters. There was video start within walking distance. His little niece wanted to go with us. Half way I had to pick her up. We made it inside the store. The store was quiet. Clenton's niece touched my face and asked, "are you black?' It got even quieter until I started laughing and answered yes. The other customers laughed. I grew to love his family as my own. Being near them without Clenton was difficult. My ill health has made me realize that I have missed making more memories with them. I hope they can forgive me, and I am praying its not too late to continue the bond.

I wake every morning missing a part of me, the best part of me. My heart lost its rhythm on July 13, 2011. God sent someone to teach it a new beat. It got out of sync when I became ill and dependent on him. Life is better in that chapter. I thank the Lord for all that has given me and for all that He has not.

This evening I received a card in the mail for a doctor I worked with. I read the note with tears in my eyes. He had sent me a blessing but called it a belated wedding gift. God is awesome. He sends angels to help me get through the darkness. It was the idea of knowing someone cared enough to write me a lovely note.

11/04/2018

I am sitting in my home office in the darkness. My mind is trying to comprehend living on a fixed income at the age of 54. My health has been my enemy for the last few years. My home needs a great deal of repair, need to purchase a vehicle, need to catch up on my personal bills, get this book published, donate to the food bank, help hubby with household bills and have money to travel. I could use my previous salary for a couple more years. It wasn't meant to be.

11/17/2018

It is difficult to believe that in a few days the smell of Thanksgiving will fill the homes of friends and family. I am not cooking this year. My sister in law invited me to join them for a noon meal. I plan to make a bacon cheese potato casserole. It has not been a good week. I am covered with poison ivy reaction. If my face doesn't clear soon, I will send hubby out with to go containers. I will stay home and watch Christmas movies or finish writing this book. However, I would much rather visit friends and family. I don't want to share my poison ivy.

11/20/2018

I had restless sleep last pm. I have one living aunt. We had gathered for her funeral. The odd thing was that those that are living were decease and those that are deceased were alive. Clenton was in my dream. I tried to catch him as he fell backwards. Our hands slipped. I found myself reaching, calling his name, sweating, crying and staring at an empty corner of my bedroom. My heart broke into a million pieces as if my mom, my sweet Clenton died last night.

My ears are listening to Pres. Trump giving his reason for not punishing Saudi Arabia for taking a human life. This doesn't make America great. California is experiencing fires that He believes it was cause by the forest staff not keeping the areas free of over growth. He has done some good but the lies and his disrespect for women of color sickens my soul. I pray every night that God will keep us safe. I believe the occurrences that happen on our life's journey is God's plan, but he gifted us the concept of choice. God must be testing humanity. There have been numerous tragedies caused by tragic souls. I wish I knew a solution. I believe in America. I respect to office of the presidency. I love our democracy and in 2020, God Bless America by giving most of us the intelligence to vote for the other person.

I apologize for getting off track with politics, I am tired of shaking my head. I feel as if the world is watching a movie about a crime ring. God will guide America and myself through this double standard madness. I am with flaws of my own, but the value of humanity is far greater than an arms deal or a dollar bill.

11-22-2018

Today is Thanksgiving. We have been invited to three homes. All of them are embedded in my heart. I made some cheesy bacon potatoes to take to Clenton's sister's home. Elrese was nervous about meeting them, although they attended our wedding. The food was delicious, and the house was filled with laughter, love and joy. I confess that I was worried that it would be awkward being there without Clenton. It felt familiar and loving. I did not feel like a stranger. Elrese said he had a nice time and looks forward to visiting them again.

We all hugged each other before we headed to my oldest sister's house in Nolanville, Texas. My legs and feet had started hurting up to a level 8. It was difficult to walk, I kept pushing myself. I was determined to spend to with all those embedded in my heart. My sister had a nice spread. It was a disappointment that I was more stuffed that every turkey in America. I couldn't take another bite of anything. We were invited to a third Thanksgiving meal and we were do some shopping. I made it to our car and I had to lift my legs with my hand. My body was ready to lay down. Elrese had pain in his back which caused us to head home for the day. I fell asleep before I could place my c-pap on my face. I didn't have any dreams just solid sleeping.

11-23-2018

Shopping at a craft store was our first stop today, grocery store was the second stop and our last stop was a fast food chicken restaurant. I finished the Chancellor Family" thankful for tree". It would have been a fuller tree had everyone been able to get together. I dislike the crowded stores, everyone is in a hurry on their time but not on mine. There are no spare seconds to locate Summer clearance items among the pumpkins, witches, turkeys, Christmas trees and valentines. What happened to celebrating one thing during its designated time of year? I guess I can score a few ceramic pumpkins for Fall 2019. I trust the Lord will gift me more time on earth.

11-25-2018

I opened my eyes this morning to view a beautiful sunrise. The wind is howling outside causing the branches on the trees to do a dance. Elrese and I are both in pain this morning. Attending worship service is still on our agenda. I also have an online order to pick up at the craft store after church. The sermon today was about living a faithful life. Trusting God more than luck or man. There is always such a warmth of love after fellowship. It does boggle my mind to know that I was 15 yrs. old when I first walked through those doors. Today I am 54yrs old. So many have gone home including Clenton. I must live a life pleasing to the Lord. I want to see my mom, Clenton, friends, family, God and Jesus. My number one goal is to please God, number two be a happiness to my spouse and number be a blessing to all those in need who cross my path.

It was beautiful to fill my faith cup again, but someone shared a stomach flu with me. I went to bed tonight, feeling exhausted and feverish. My head and body ached all night. Sleeping was not part of my nighttime.

I threw up what little I had taken in during the day. It was coming out of both ends. I would sweat then shiver. It was a long night.

11-29-2018

A friend was running errands this am, so I got dressed to catch a ride. I really need to get my own vehicle soon. I am trapped at home unless someone makes time for me. I don't have health insurance now, so I canceled my upcoming appointments. I rescheduled them for January. I am more worried about unable to purchase my medications without insurance. I am stress eating all day and I feel like a caged animal stranded in the middle of nowhere. I enjoyed hanging out with my friend. It was windy, but it felt like a Spring day instead of a Fall day.

Hubby put up our Christmas tree. It remains UN-decorated. I think after he comes from his movie afternoon Saturday, we shall get it decorated. This year has become filled with blurred memories of surgeries, hospital stays, and doctor office visits. I trust if God gifts me 2019, the year will be better. My health; psychical, financial and spiritual will be fantastic. The month of December begins in 2 days. My mood will improve after I get all my Christmas greeting cards sent and present wrapped. I love the spirit of the season. Kindness and hope permeate the air.

The last few weeks I have been trying to reconnect with people from my earlier years. It is exhausting and discouraging. No one writes me back. So, I will just move on. They know where I am located. The friends that are in my life at present is enough. Most people drift in and out of my life. I know who the real people are as well as the users. I show them all love especially the users. I am not perfect, and I will never claim to be perfect. I am a proudly flawed human being who works hard at being kind.

Retirement

Many people work their whole career looking forward to retirement.
Youth falsely told me I would work until I was ninety-nine
Reality informed me that my body was struggling at 50.
I pushed with every ounce of strength
Now I am being pushed in wheelchairs, stretchers and hospital beds.
sitting waiting for life to happen on the television is like death
The silence is worst, it's like screaming but no sound is heard.
I miss the connection with my teammates, my work family.
Some days I feel as if I am exiled on a deserted island
Some days I breathe a sigh of relief because I can roll over and go back to sleep.
I don't want my sunset to be filled with boredom or hospital stays.
Life can change so quickly but I must keep pushing up the hill.
Retirement isn't death, it's a change of necessity.
Embracing this part of my journey is not easy but I shall conquer it.
I will dance in the rain, sing out loud and laugh until it hurts.

Wind

Lying in bed listening to the howling wind,
Brings forth memories of hopes that end.
Howling louder with each gust,
Tears begin to fall from my eyes as they must.
My heart loves another but misses you still.
The howling wind sings the song of memories,
Haunting my thoughts, oh how I miss you.
I cannot dwell in the past,
If I want my new love to last.

This journey I am traveling is about more than myself. It is about making a positive difference in this world of humans I will leave with you some words of wisdom. Before you go to sleep at night, tell your spouse how important he/she is and talk to God together. Be kind to everyone who crosses your path. Be selfless and love like Jesus loved. Don't worry about the tomorrows because God has them covered. Be Blessed and be a blessing.

Christmas 2018

The lights are not shining bright enough,
The darkness of depression over shadows.
The many packages don't bring me peace.
Next year will be better, maybe.
It must be because this year was not a winner.
I am alive, God embraced me with love.
This year could have been worse.
If I see next Christmas, there will be a smaller tree,
Less ribbon and bows.
More quality time and peace.

Christmas afternoon Elrese and I went to break bread at my sister's home. We can't all be together for the holidays, but it sure is nice to spend time with family. The food was delicious, and the love of family is priceless. I wish we would have family dinners every Saturday evening I wish a great number of things. I wish we could stop time. I wish we could go back in time, not to change moments but to feel childlike innocence once more.

Today I had my first doctor visit in 2019. My doctor told me I was a strong woman because I have been through a great deal. Only time will tell. The passage of time, of life is a series of events that cause us to re-invent ourselves in order to move forward. My circumstances are the death of my first spouse, the death of my mother, my new marriage, the failing of my health and the necessary retirement. My life has not been all smooth roads but I know without any doubt I have been blessed.

Random Pieces

An unread handwritten note hidden between the pages of time,
Could it be one last "I love you"
Photographs faded and new, captured the life we had
Random pieces we leave behind not to be
Memories of a tender touch,
Memories of a soft kiss
Random pieces we leave behind to comfort and remind us of hopeful
bliss.
Random pieces of a legacy whether it be large or small
Random pieces we leave behind.

Printed in the United States
By Bookmasters